MOVING UP WITH SCIENCE

ROCKS AND SOIL

Peter Riley

W

FRANKLIN WATTS

LONDON • SYDNEY

To my granddaughter, Holly Jane.

First published in 2015 by
Franklin Watts
338 Euston Road
London NW1 3BH

Franklin Watts Australia
Level 17/207 Kent Street
Sydney NSW 2000

HB ISBN: 978 1 4451 3514 4
Library ebook ISBN: 978 1 4451 3515 1

Dewey classification number: 552

A CIP catalogue record for this book is available from the British Library.

Editor: Hayley Fairhead
Designer: Elaine Wilkinson

Photo acknowledgments: BluesandViews p7b; Rasmus Holmboe Dahl p12; Elena Elisseeva p16r; Hans Engbers p24; Santiago Rodríguez Fontoba p8; Henrik_L p20; Vivian Mcaleavey p13; Ivan Nakonechnyy p19 pxhidalgo p9; Daniel Schreiber p11; Marcio Silva p25; Straga p15; Kheng Ho Toh p16l; Anthony Aneese Totah Jr p27; Trondur title page and p10; Derek Trott p5b; Shevelev Vladimir p17; Webspark p6; Juergen Weidmann p21 and p31; Michael Wood p14b.

Artwork: John Alston

All other photographs by Leon Hargreaves.
With thanks to our models Sebastian Smith-Beatty and Sofia Bottomley.

Franklin Watts is a division of Hachette Children's Books, an Hachette UK company.
www.hachette.co.uk

Printed in China

Contents

Words in **bold** can be found in the glossary on pages 28–29.

Rocks in space

The Earth is a rocky planet, but where did the rocks come from?

How Earth began

Around 4.6 **billion** years ago a cloud of **gas** and dust swirled about in space. The gas came together and formed a **star** – our Sun. The dust **particles** crashed into each other and formed small pieces of rock, like **gravel.** These small pieces of rock crashed together and formed bigger lumps of rock, like boulders. These boulders crashed together and got bigger and bigger until, after millions of years, the Earth was formed. The dust particles crashed together to make other rocky planets too. These are Mercury, Venus and Mars.

Try the following experiment to show how a cloud of dust can make a rocky planet.

Equipment:

- Ten tiny balls of modelling clay •
- Ten medium-sized balls of modelling clay, ten times larger than the original balls
- Ten large balls of modelling clay, ten times larger again

1.
Add the ten tiny balls together to make one ball, then add this ball to one of the medium-sized balls. Add this ball to all the other nine medium-sized balls.

2.
Add the ball they make to one of the large balls. Add all the large balls together to make your model planet.

Asteroid belt

Some lumps of rock stopped crashing together and made **asteroids**. Asteroids form a huge belt around the rocky planets.

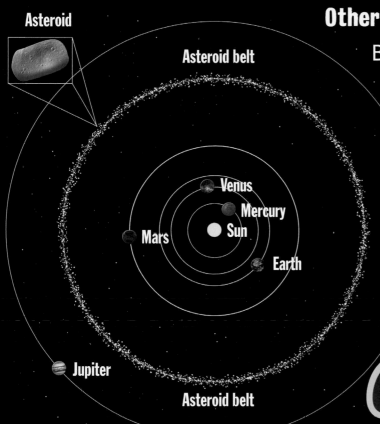

Asteroid

Asteroid belt

Venus

Mercury

Sun

Mars

Earth

Jupiter

Asteroid belt

Other planets

Beyond the asteroid belt, lumps of rocks formed the centre of other planets in our **Solar System**. These planets have **liquids** and gases around their rocky centres. They are Jupiter, Saturn, Uranus and Neptune.

Many planets have **moons** around them. These are also made of rock.

Where do you find rocks in the Solar System?

5

Inside the Earth

If you could slice open the Earth you would find that it has four parts. The part which forms the surface is called the **crust**. Beneath this is the **mantle**, and below the mantle are the outer **core** and inner core.

Different layers

The outer core is made from very hot liquid metal. The inner core is made from a huge metal ball that spins in the liquid. The Earth's mantle is made of hot rock but the rock does not stay still. It moves very slowly under the Earth's crust.

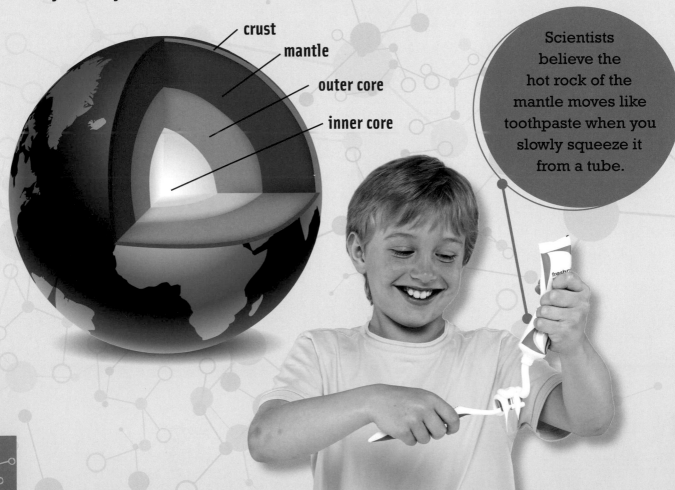

crust

mantle

outer core

inner core

Scientists believe the hot rock of the mantle moves like toothpaste when you slowly squeeze it from a tube.

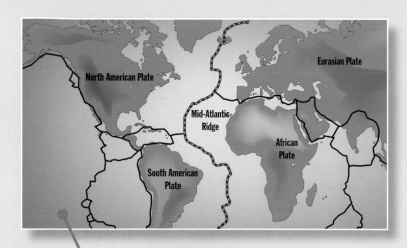

Earth's moving crust

The Earth's crust is made from a few huge slabs of rock called plates. They make up the land and the floors of the seas.

As the mantle moves it makes the slabs in the crust move. When the edges of the slabs rub together they make the crust shake. We call this shaking an earthquake. The slab of crust you are on now is moving very slowly. It is moving at the speed your fingernails are growing.

This world map shows the black outline of each plate on the Earth's crust, where earthquakes are most likely to happen.

These buildings in Christchurch, New Zealand were damaged by an earthquake in 2011.

How fast are your fingernails growing? Ask an adult to cut your fingernails. Check them every few days to see how far the white part has grown over your fingertip.

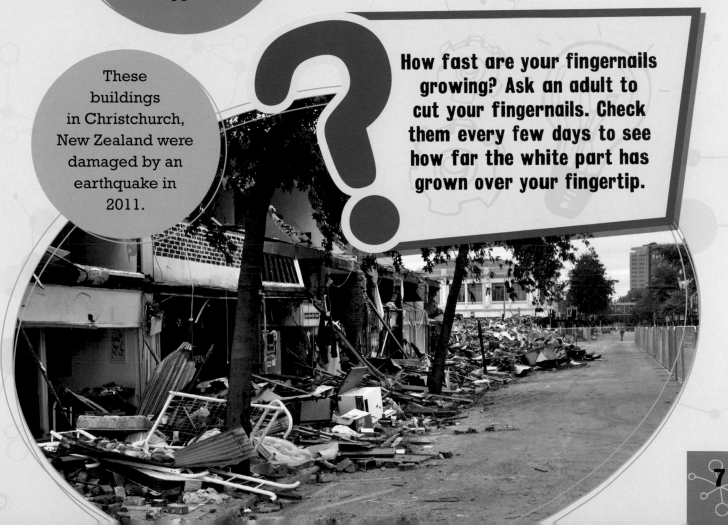

Volcanoes

The rock in the Earth's mantle is much hotter than the rock in the crust. In some places the hot mantle rock pushes up through cracks in the crust. This rock is called **magma**. It comes out of the crust at a **volcano**. There are two main types of volcano – shield volcanoes and cone-shaped volcanoes.

Shield volcanoes

When a shield volcano **erupts**, the magma flows out and forms a liquid rock called **lava**. This cools down to make solid rock. The lava flows quickly and travels for long distances before it cools. This gives shield volcanoes gently sloping sides.

El Teide in Tenerife, Canary Islands is a shield volcano.

Tungurahua in Ecuador is a cone-shaped volcano. When it erupts, steam, ash, gas and rocks shoot high into the air.

Cone-shaped volcanoes

Underneath a cone-shaped volcano, the magma builds up until it forces itself out in a great explosion. The erupting volcano shoots smelly gases, steam, ash and large rocks, called volcanic bombs, high into the air.

The steam, ash and gases form a cloud that settles over the land, while lava flows out of the top of the cone. When this lava cools down it forms solid rock.

Soil from volcanic rock

Some volcanoes have not erupted for a long time. They are called **extinct** volcanoes. Over thousands of years the rocks from the volcanoes break down to make a rich soil which farmers use to grow their crops.

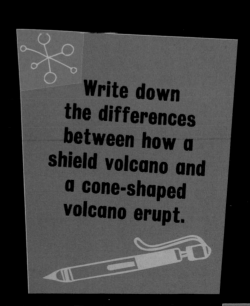

Write down the differences between how a shield volcano and a cone-shaped volcano erupt.

Igneous rock

Igneous rock is made from the magma under the Earth's crust. When a volcano erupts the magma forms lava, which flows away from the volcano and begins to cool. When lava cools down it forms rock made of very small **grains**. Basalt is the most common type of volcanic rock.

Basalt is a dark rock that can form columns in the shape of hexagons, like these rocks from the Giant's Causeway in Northern Ireland.

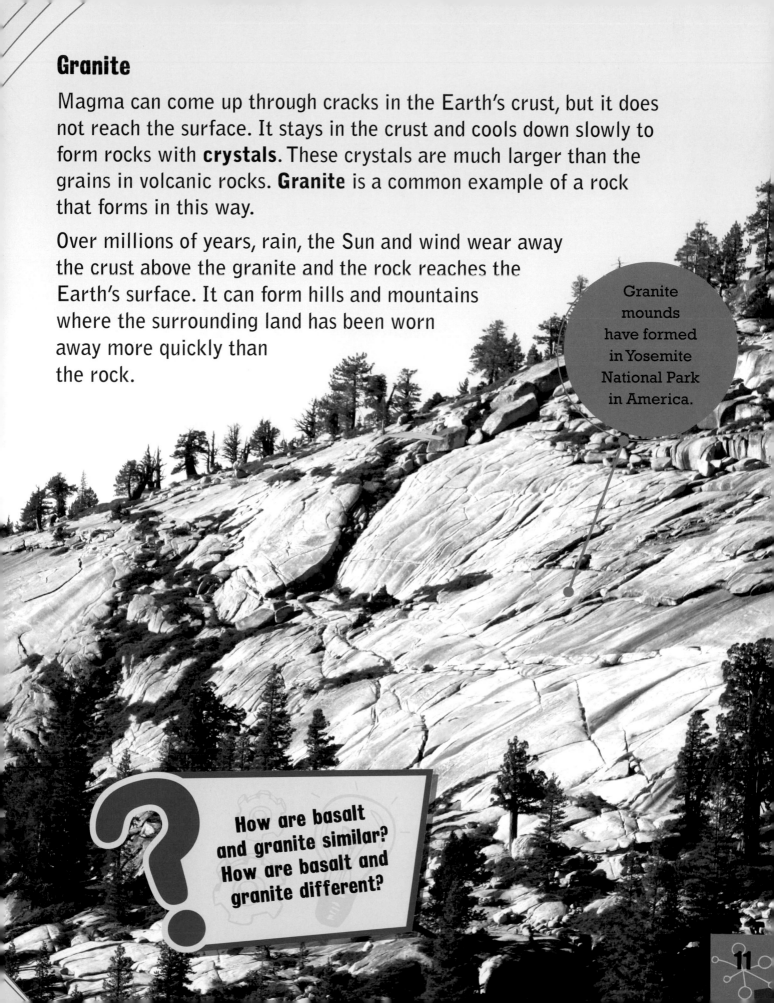

Granite

Magma can come up through cracks in the Earth's crust, but it does not reach the surface. It stays in the crust and cools down slowly to form rocks with **crystals**. These crystals are much larger than the grains in volcanic rocks. **Granite** is a common example of a rock that forms in this way.

Over millions of years, rain, the Sun and wind wear away the crust above the granite and the rock reaches the Earth's surface. It can form hills and mountains where the surrounding land has been worn away more quickly than the rock.

Granite mounds have formed in Yosemite National Park in America.

How are basalt and granite similar? How are basalt and granite different?

When rocks break up

Rocks on the Earth's surface are broken down by the weather. This process is called weathering. Rain **dissolves** some of the rocks. The Sun's heat makes the rocks swell a little and crack. Rainwater freezes in the cracks and the ice pushes on the sides and breaks up the rock.

Erosion

The pieces of broken rock are washed away by the rain or blown by the wind. This moving away of the rocky fragments is called **erosion**.

It's not just the weather that can cause rocks to break up. The pounding waves of the sea have worn down and cracked these rocks over millions of years.

Sedimentary rocks

Tiny grains of rock which have been washed away by the rain settle downriver in lakes and seas. When rock grains settle underwater they form a **sediment**. The grains of sediment pile up to form a layer. In time the layer gets thicker and thicker. It gets so thick that it is squashed by its own weight. This turns the rock grains into a layer of solid rock. All rocks which have formed from layers of grains are called sedimentary rock.

Sand grains have settled to form these layers of a sedimentary rock called sandstone.

Describe one way in which the weather can affect rocks.

Rocks from living things

Some sedimentary rocks form from the shells of living things that lived in seas millions of years ago. When the creatures died, their empty shells settled on the sea floor and formed a layer which eventually turned into rock.

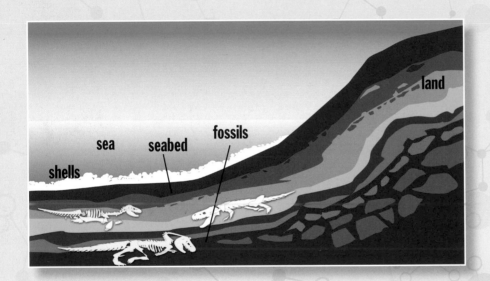

shells

sea

seabed

fossils

land

Limestone

Limestone is a hard, white or grey rock. It is made from the shells of sea creatures, such as snails, clams and crinoids that lived millions of years ago.

A crinoid has feeding arms and a stalk which holds it in the water.

Coal

Millions of years ago there were huge **swamps** on the Earth. Massive trees grew in them. When the trees died they fell into the swamps. Over time, the trees turned into a hard, black rock called coal.

Today coal is dug out of the dried-up swamps and burnt in power stations to make electricity.

Chalk

Chalk is made from the shells of very tiny living things that floated in the sea millions of years ago. When they died the shells sank to the sea floor and packed together to make a soft, white rock called chalk.

Describe how chalk is different from coal.

15

Minerals

All rocks are made of **minerals**. Minerals are made from **chemicals** in the ground that link together and can form crystals. The crystals have different shapes, such as cubes or hexagons, and come in a variety of colours. They join together to form many different kinds of rock.

Gemstones

Some minerals have attractive colours and some sparkle when light shines on them. These minerals are called gemstones. They can be used to make jewellery. In a diamond, a chemical called carbon links together to make a hard, clear crystal. Diamonds are so strong they can be used to cut hard materials.

These rocks containing diamonds have been discovered inside a mine.

A geode is a hollow rock in which large crystals are formed.

You can see large crystals in granite. Granite is made from a pink mineral called feldspar, a black mineral called mica and a white mineral called quartz.

Mineral crystals

In most rocks the minerals grow into each other. You cannot easily see their separate crystal shapes because they are locked together, making the rocks hard and strong.

Some mineral crystals, such as calcite, are so small you can only see them with a **microscope**. The shells of sea animals are made from calcite. This makes the shells hard, protecting the animal inside.

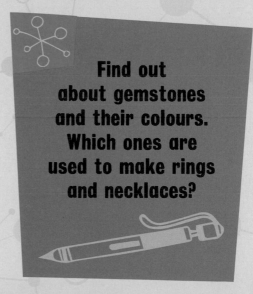

Find out about gemstones and their colours. Which ones are used to make rings and necklaces?

Metamorphic rock

Metamorphic rock forms from another type of rock. Heat and pressure inside the Earth's crust can cause a rock to change. For example, this happens when two plates in the Earth's crust push together to form mountains.

Inside mountains, the Earth's plates push together, making the rocks change.

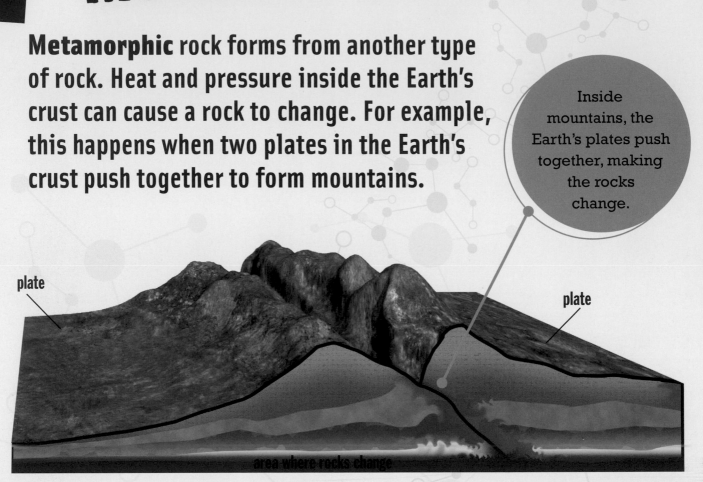

plate

plate

area where rocks change

Slate

Shale is a sedimentary rock. Its mineral crystals are locked together in all directions. When the Earth's plates push together the increase in heat and pressure makes these minerals change and line up in rows. This change creates a new waterproof rock called slate. The rows of minerals make slate break up into sheets when it is hit with a hammer. Slate is a hard rock which can be used in buildings for roof and floor tiles.

Marble

Sometimes magma flows up inside cracks in the crust. It heats the rock next to the cracks and changes it.

When magma heats up limestone, it changes it into a metamorphic rock called marble. Marble is a very hard, smooth rock that can look sparkly like sugar. Clay and sand mixed in with the limestone changes too, making coloured lines in the marble called veins.

This **sculpture** of a lion has been made from marble.

? Why do you think slate is used to make roofs and marble is used to make sculptures?

Soil

Soil forms from rock and living things. Wind, rain and ice break down rock into sand, silt and clay (see page 12). The remains of dead plants and animals are broken down by **bacteria** and insects to form **humus**. Humus mixes with the sand, silt and clay and gives the soil its dark colour.

Woodlice feed on dead trees and break them down into humus.

Rich waste

Manure from animals forms humus in the soil. Gardeners and farmers use manure to help plants and crops to grow.

There are different types of soil:

Sandy soils

Sand particles are large and have big air spaces between them. Water can move through these spaces quickly and drain away.

Clay soils

Clay particles are very small and have very small air spaces between them. Water cannot pass through these spaces quickly and is held back above the soil.

Loam soils

Loam is a soil with a mixture of humus, sand, silt and clay. The humus binds the rocky particles together to make large crumbs which help the soil drain well.

Gardeners use a loam soil like this one for growing plants.

Do you think loam has small or large air spaces? Explain your answer.

Investigating soil

Sofia and Seb have two samples of dry soil. They examine them with magnifying glasses. They see that soil A has larger soil particles than soil B. Seb says that soil A will have larger air spaces between the particles and so it will drain water faster than soil B. Sofia and Seb decide to test Seb's idea.

Equipment:

- 2 x types of soil (A and B) • 2 x funnels • stopwatch • cotton wool
- 2 x plastic bottles • water • 2 x measuring cylinders

1.
Seb and Sofia put a little plug of cotton wool in each funnel and place each funnel in the top of two plastic bottles.

2.
Seb and Sofia put the same amount of soil in each funnel.

3.
Sofia uses a measuring cylinder to pour the same amount of water into each funnel while Seb starts the stopwatch for two minutes.

4.
Seb and Sofia compare the amount of drained water by pouring it into their measuring cylinders.

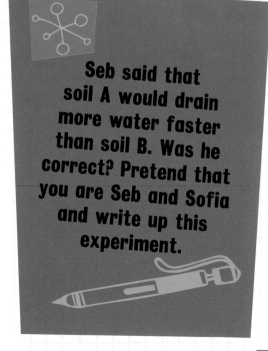

Seb said that soil A would drain more water faster than soil B. Was he correct? Pretend that you are Seb and Sofia and write up this experiment.

23

How fossils form

Fossils are formed from animals and plants that lived long ago. When these animals and plants died they did not form humus because they were quickly covered with sand or mud. This stopped other living things feeding on them and breaking down their bodies.

The effect of water

Over time the sand and mud turned into rock. Water passing through the rock dissolved some of its minerals. When the water reached the hard parts of the buried plant or animal, the minerals became solid again. They turned the hard parts of the dead animals and plants into fossils.

Fossil skeleton of a Tyrannosaurus-Rex that lived over 65 million years ago.

This fossil has formed from a fish that died and was covered with sand. The sand settled over the fish and turned it to stone.

Finding fossils

Sometimes **trace fossils** form. Examples of trace fossils are animal tracks, dinosaur eggs and the prints of leaves in a rock.

In time the rocks above a fossil may be worn away by the weather. This uncovers the fossil and makes it easier to find. Fossils are collected by scientists who study them to find out about living things in the past.

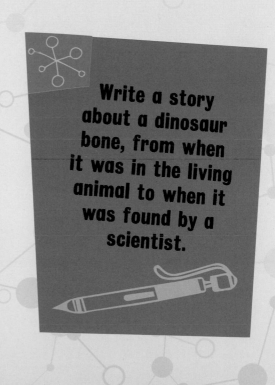

Write a story about a dinosaur bone, from when it was in the living animal to when it was found by a scientist.

Fossils from different ages

Fossils form in sedimentary rocks like sandstone and limestone. Over millions of years, layers of these rocks have been created in the Earth's crust.

Earth's layers

The oldest layers are the deepest and the youngest layers are at the top. Each layer has been given a name and scientists have worked out its age. Contained in each layer are many fossils. Scientists are able to tell the first time a type of animal or plant was present on Earth by the layer in which is was found.

Name of layer	Time when the layer was made	Fossil plants and animals found
Quarternary	1.6 million years ago	First humans
Tertiary	65 million years ago	First **mammals**
Cretaceous	135 million years ago	End of dinosaurs
Jurassic	205 million years ago	First birds, first flowering plants
Triassic	250 million years ago	First dinosaurs
Permian	300 million years ago	Lots of **amphibians** and **conifer trees**. End of **trilobites**
Carboniferous	355 million years ago	First **reptiles**, first insects with wings, lots of ferns
Devonian	410 million years ago	Lots of fish, first amphibians
Silurian	435 million years ago	First centipedes and millipedes
Ordovician	510 million years ago	First **corals**, first land plants
Cambrian	570 million years ago	Trilobites, first **molluscs**
Precambrian	Before 570 million years ago	**Microbes** and **sponges**

Extinction

Some fossils appear in older layers but not in newer layers. This means that the plants or animals that made them have died out or become extinct. The dinosaurs became extinct at the end of the Cretaceous, 65 million years ago.

Small sea creatures called trilobites became extinct at the end of the Permian, over 250 million years ago.

In which rock layers can you find fossils of the first mammals, the first birds and the first land plants? Put them in order, starting with the oldest.

Evolution

Fossils show how one kind of living thing can change into another. For example, scientists believe that some ancient fish changed slightly every time a new fish was born. Over millions of years, these changes created the first amphibians. The first fish fossils appear in older layers while the first amphibian fossils appear in younger layers. This changing of living things over long periods of time is called **evolution**.

Glossary

Amphibian an animal that spends its early life as a tadpole in water and its later life as a land animal such as a frog or toad.

Asteroid a piece of rock as small as a grain of sand or as large as 940km across, which is moving around the Sun like the planets in the Solar System.

Bacteria tiny living things which belong to a group called microorganisms or microbes.

Billion a thousand million.

Chemical one of many different materials that form solids, liquids and gases. Some examples are: iron, a chemical which makes up a solid; water, a chemical which makes a liquid; carbon dioxide, a chemical which forms the gas you breathe out.

Conifer trees trees with long green needles that grow cones to make seeds.

Coral small jellyfish-type animals which live together and make tubes of hard rock around themselves.

Core the centre of an object such as a planet or a fruit.

Crust the outer layer of rock on the Earth which forms the Earth's surface.

Crystal a solid with the chemicals arranged in a way that makes the sides flat and forms shapes such as cubes or oblongs.

Dissolve when a solid breaks up into tiny pieces in a liquid and seems to disappear into it.

Erosion the breaking up of rocks into smaller pieces by the weather or ocean waves.

Erupt to let out lava and gases from inside the Earth.

Evolution a process in which living things change from one kind to another over a very long time.

Extinct a kind of plant or animal that is no longer living on the Earth. Only its fossils remain. An extinct volcano is no longer active.

Fossil the remains of a plant or animal that have turned into stone.

Gases substances which do not have any shape and can spread out in the air.

Grain a very small piece of rock such as a grain of sand.

Granite a rock that forms inside the crust which is made of feldspar, mica and quartz.

Gravel a small piece of rock.

Humus a dark spongy substance in the soil, formed from the rotted remains of plants and animals.

Igneous a rock that forms from magma.

Lava a liquid which flows away from volcanoes and cools to form solid rock.

Liquid a substance that takes up the shape of its container and can flow from one place to another.

Magma molten rock which forms in the mantle.

Mammal an animal with a backbone and hair which feeds on milk from its mother.

Mantle a layer of slowly moving hot rock below the Earth's crust.

Manure the solid waste produced by animals that is used to help plants grow.

Metamorphic something that changes from one form to another.

Microbe a group of very tiny living things, also known as microorganisms.

Microscope a scientific instrument which makes objects appear bigger.

Mineral a solid that forms in the ground from a group of chemicals that link together, often forming crystals.

Mollusc an animal with a soft body, no legs and which often has a shell, such as a snail.

Moon a large, usually round object which moves around a planet.

Particle a very small piece of a solid.

Planet a large round object which moves in an orbit around the Sun or another star.

Reptile a land animal with skin covered in scales.

Sculpture an object made by carving rock or wood.

Sediment a layer at the bottom of a liquid which forms from tiny solid particles that were floating in it.

Solar System the Sun, planets, moons and asteroids.

Sponge an animal which stays in one place and draws water through the tiny holes in its body to help it feed.

Star a huge ball of gases that gives out heat and light.

Swamp a piece of land soaked with water, often found next to a pond or lake.

Trace fossils fossils made by a plant or an animal, like a track or print.

Trilobite an extinct animal that looked rather like the woodlice we see today.

Volcano an opening in the Earth's crust which releases lava, rocks and hot gases from inside the Earth.

Answers to the activities and questions

Page 5 Rocks in space

Answer: The planets Mercury, Venus, Earth and Mars are made out of rocks. The asteroids and the centres of Jupiter, Saturn, Uranus and Neptune are made out of rocks, as are all of the moons.

Page 7 Inside the Earth

Activity: Have your fingernails cut back to your finger tips. Let them grow for a week or more and measure with a ruler how far each nail has grown over your fingertip. Fingernails may grow 3mm or more in a month.

Page 9 Volcanoes

Answer: When a shield volcano erupts the lava flows out. When a cone-shaped volcano erupts out shoot smelly gases, steam, ash, volcanic bombs; and lava flows away.

Page 11 Igneous rock

Answer: Basalt and granite are similar because they both come from hot rock under the Earth's crust. Basalt and granite are different because basalt comes from volcanoes and is black. It is made from tiny grains packed together and can form rock hexagons. Granite forms in the crust and is made of crystals.

Page 13 When rocks break up

Activity: It breaks up the rock into tiny pieces called fragments and scatters them in the wind or washes them away in rain water.

Page 15 Rocks from living things

Activity: Chalk is a white rock made from the shells of microorganisms that lived in the sea long ago. Coal is black rock made from trees which fell into swamps but did not rot away.

Page 17 Minerals

Activity: Garnet (red), amethyst (pink), aquamarine (pale blue), diamond (colourless), emerald (green), ruby (red), peridot (green/yellow), sapphire (blue), opal (blue with a green sheen), topaz (orange), turquoise (light blue). Pearl is a white gemstone made by shellfish, such as oysters.

Page 19 Metamorphic rock

Answer: Slate is waterproof and makes thin sheets that can be put on a roof. Marble is sparkly and has coloured veins in it that make carved objects look attractive.

Page 21 Soil

Answer: It has large air spaces. Sand particles are large and sandy soil drains water quickly. Crumbs are large soil particles so they will have large air spaces between them.

Page 23 Investigating soil

Answer: Seb's idea is correct. You can see from the measuring cylinders that the one collecting water from soil A contains much more water than soil B.

My experiment
I collected two funnels and put a little plug of cotton wool in each of them. I put each funnel in the top of a plastic bottle. I put an amount of soil A in one funnel and the same amount of soil B in the second funnel. I poured the same amount of water into each funnel, started the stopwatch and let it run for two minutes, then stopped the water draining by taking the funnels out of the bottles. I poured the water from each bottle into two measuring cylinders to find out how much each soil had drained. I found that more water had passed through soil A than soil B. I concluded that soil A drains water faster than B.

Page 25 How fossils form

Activity: Here is an example of a story about a dinosaur bone: The dinosaur became ill and died. It fell into mud and was quickly covered up with more mud as the river flowed over it. In time the mud changed into rock. Water passing down through the rock dissolved some of the minerals, but when they reached the dinosaur bones the minerals formed solids inside the bones. More time went by and the rocks above the dinosaur bones were worn away by the weather. The dinosaur bones stuck out of the Earth's surface. A scientist found them.

Page 27 Fossils from different ages

In order of oldest first:
First land plants: Ordovician layer
First birds: Jurassic layer
First mammals: Tertiary layer

Index

About this book

Moving Up with Science is designed to help children develop the following skills:

Science enquiry skills: researching using secondary sources, all pages but specifically the further research project on page 17; observing over time, page 7; comparative or fair test, page 23.

Working scientifically: making careful observations, pages 7 and 17; making a comparative or fair test, page 23; using results to draw simple conclusions, page 23; using straightforward scientific evidence to answer questions, pages 7 and 17.

Critical thinking skills: knowledge, page 5; comprehension, pages 13 and 21; analysis, pages 9, 11, 15, 19, 23 and 27; synthesis, page 25; evaluate, page 27.